This Book

Belongs to :

....

....

Mosaics Art

Relaxation coloring book

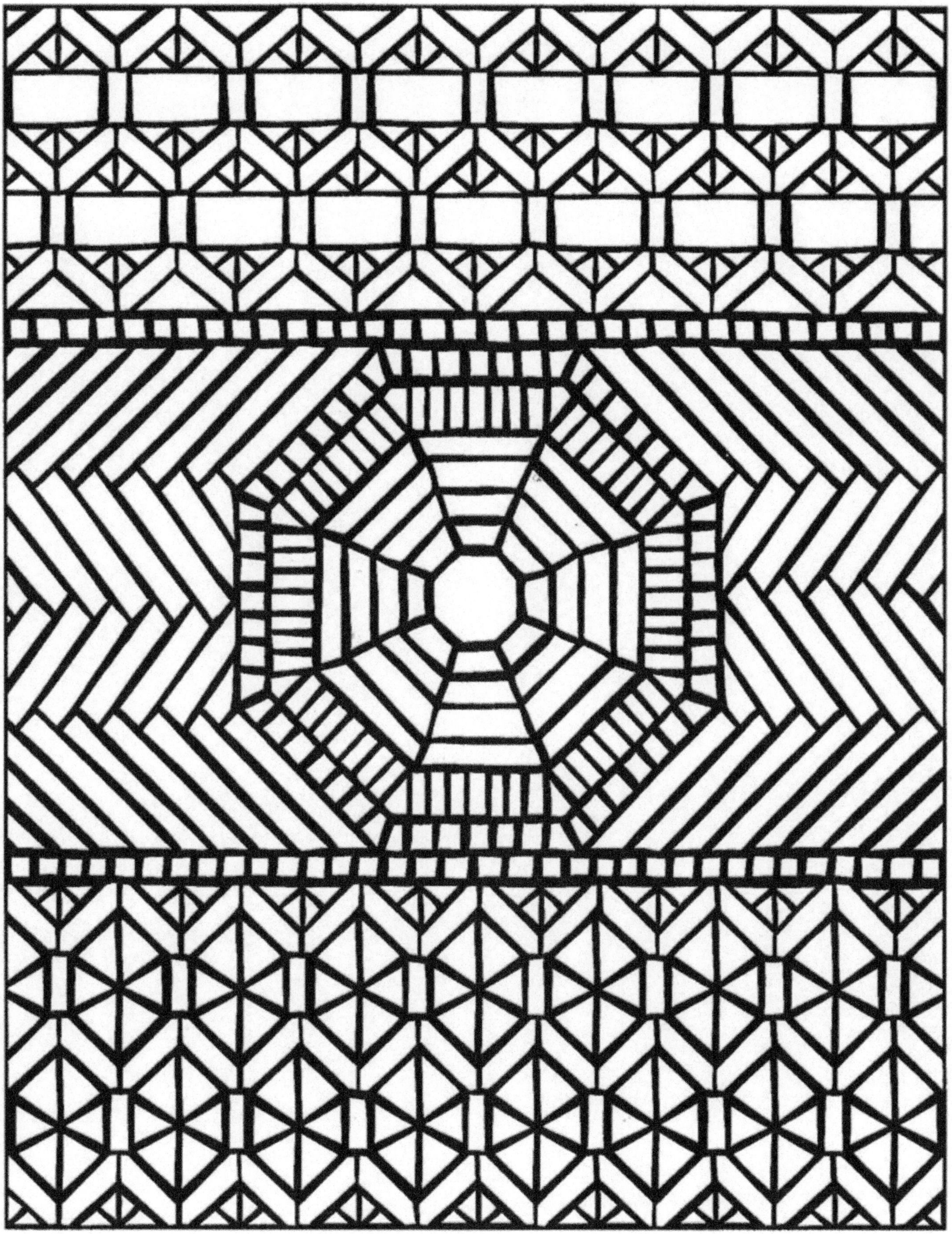

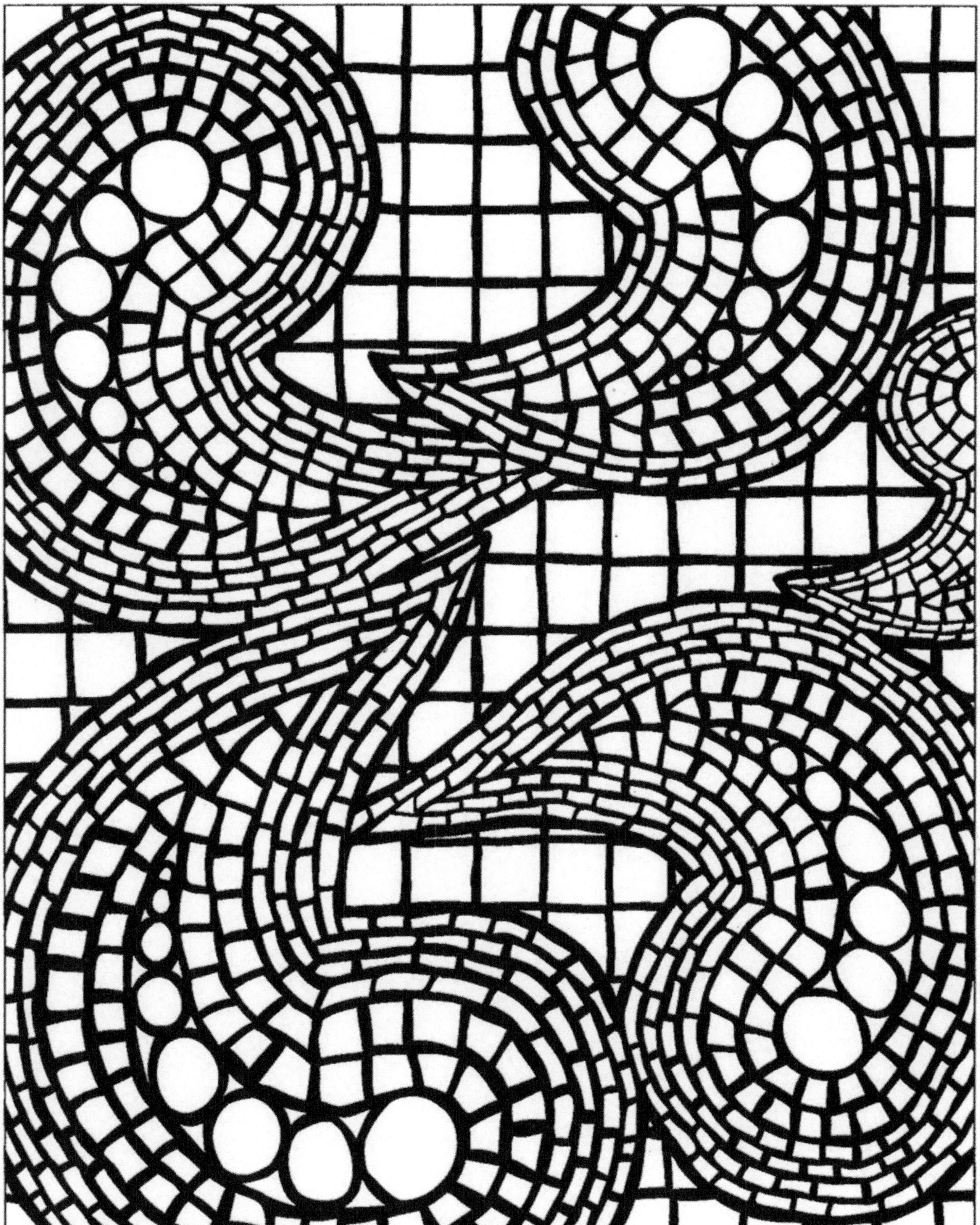

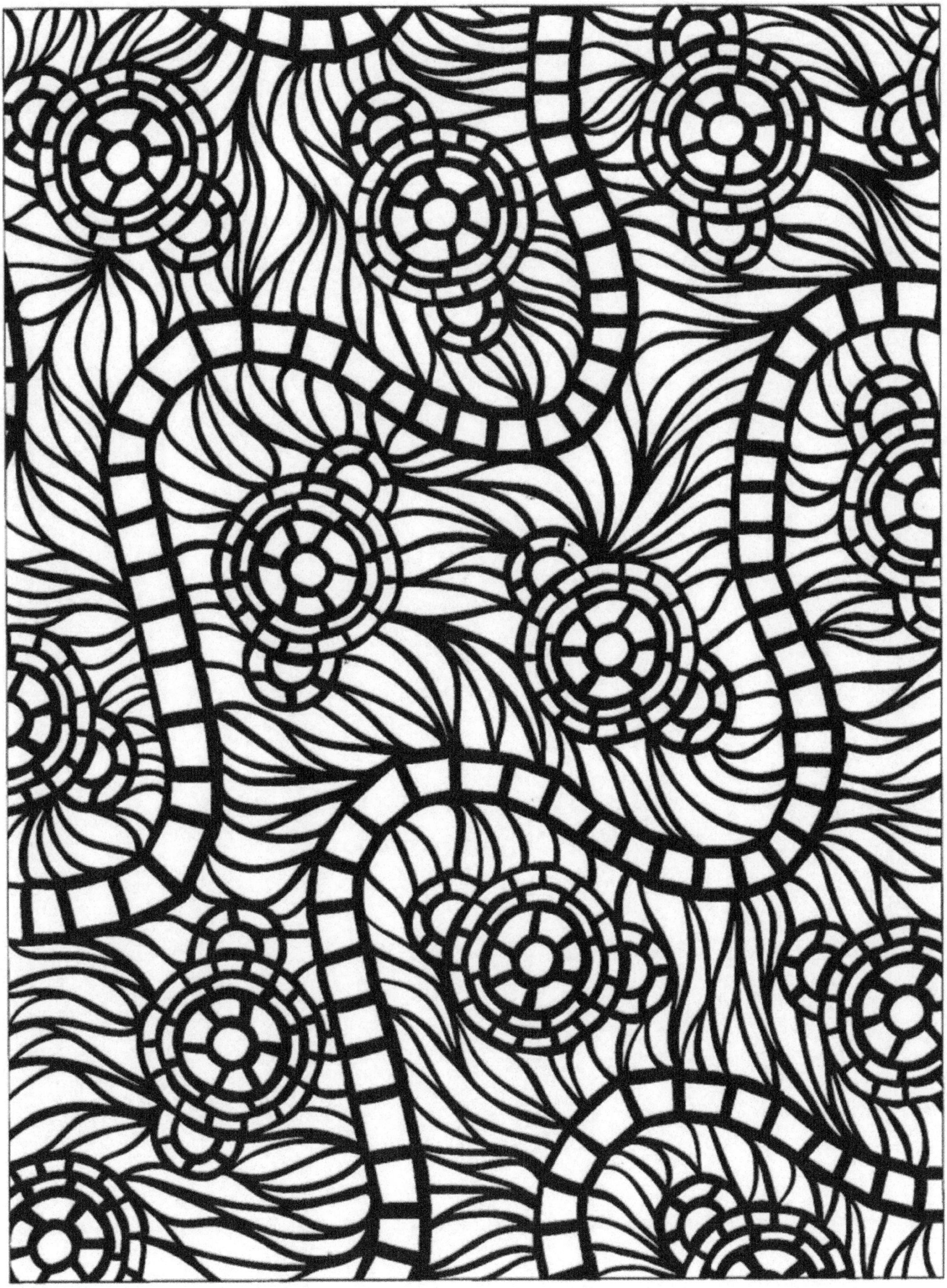

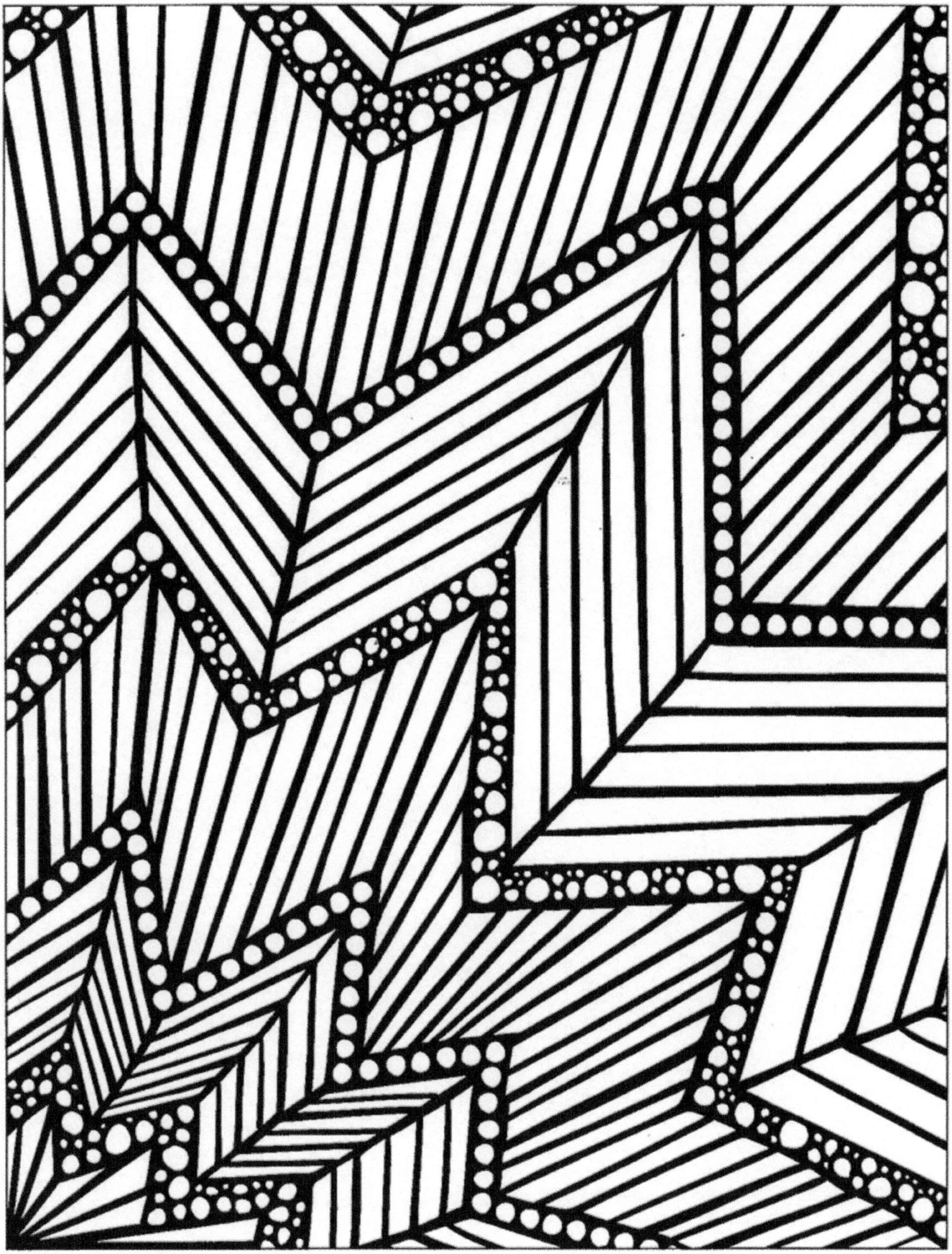

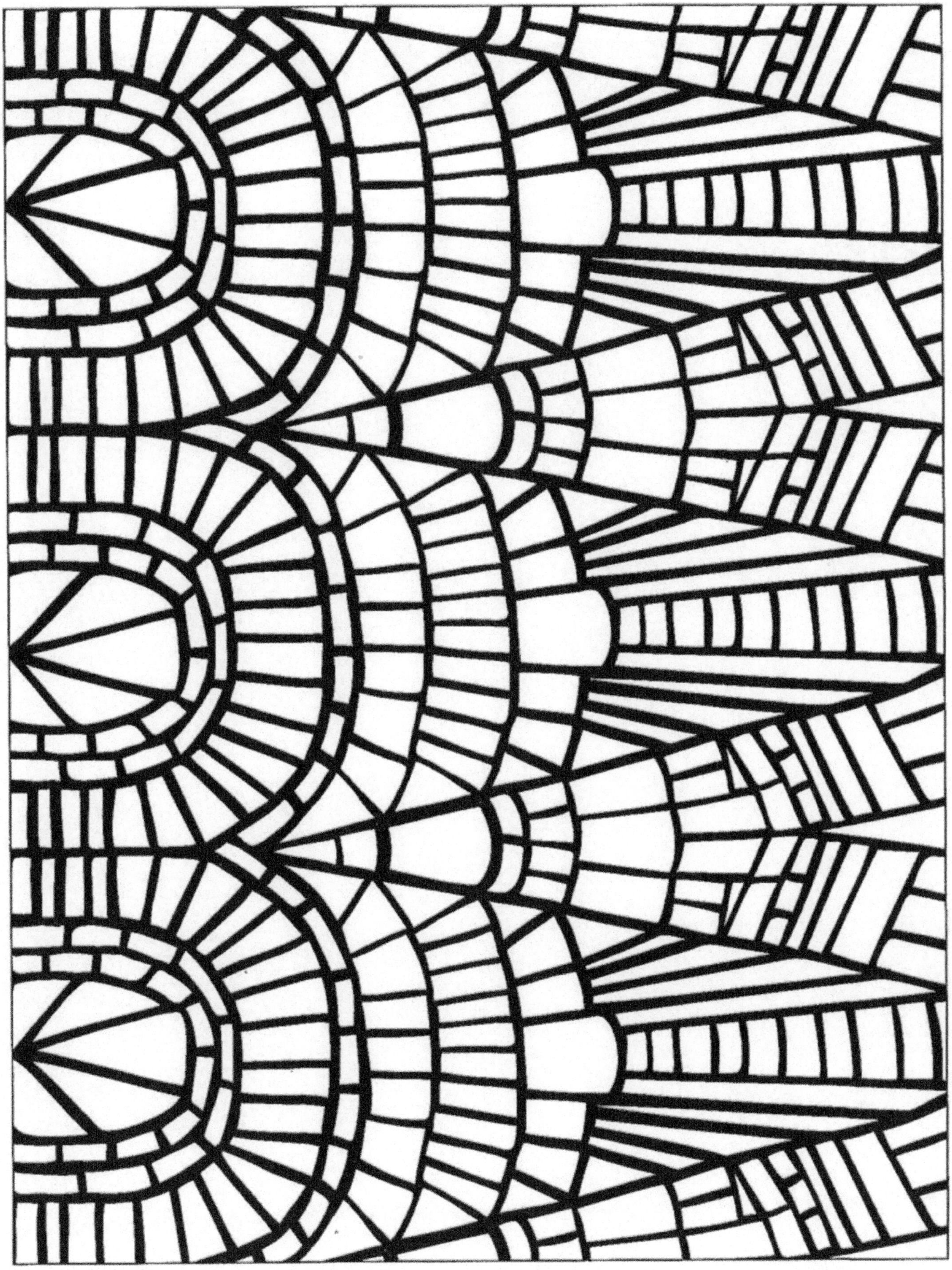

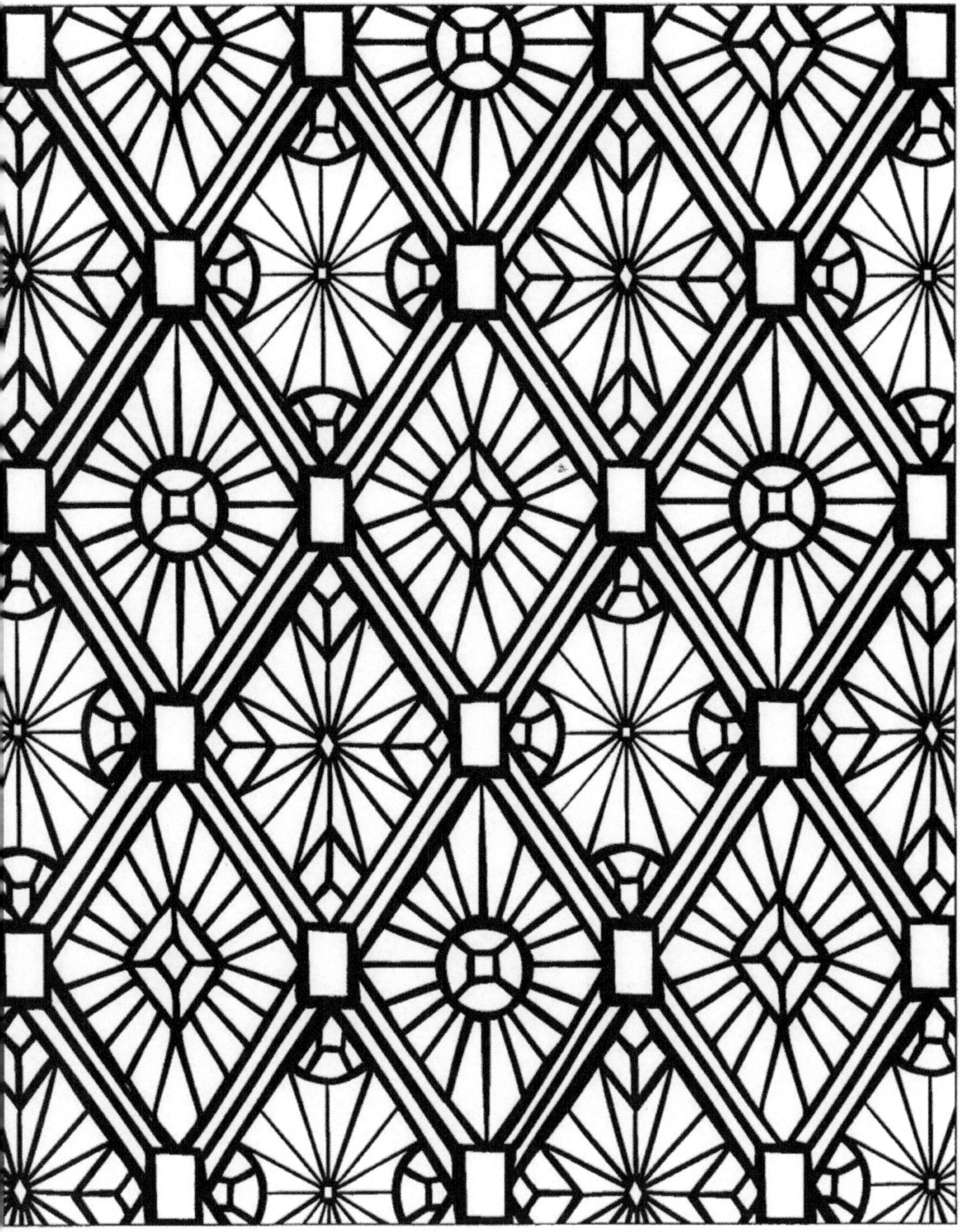

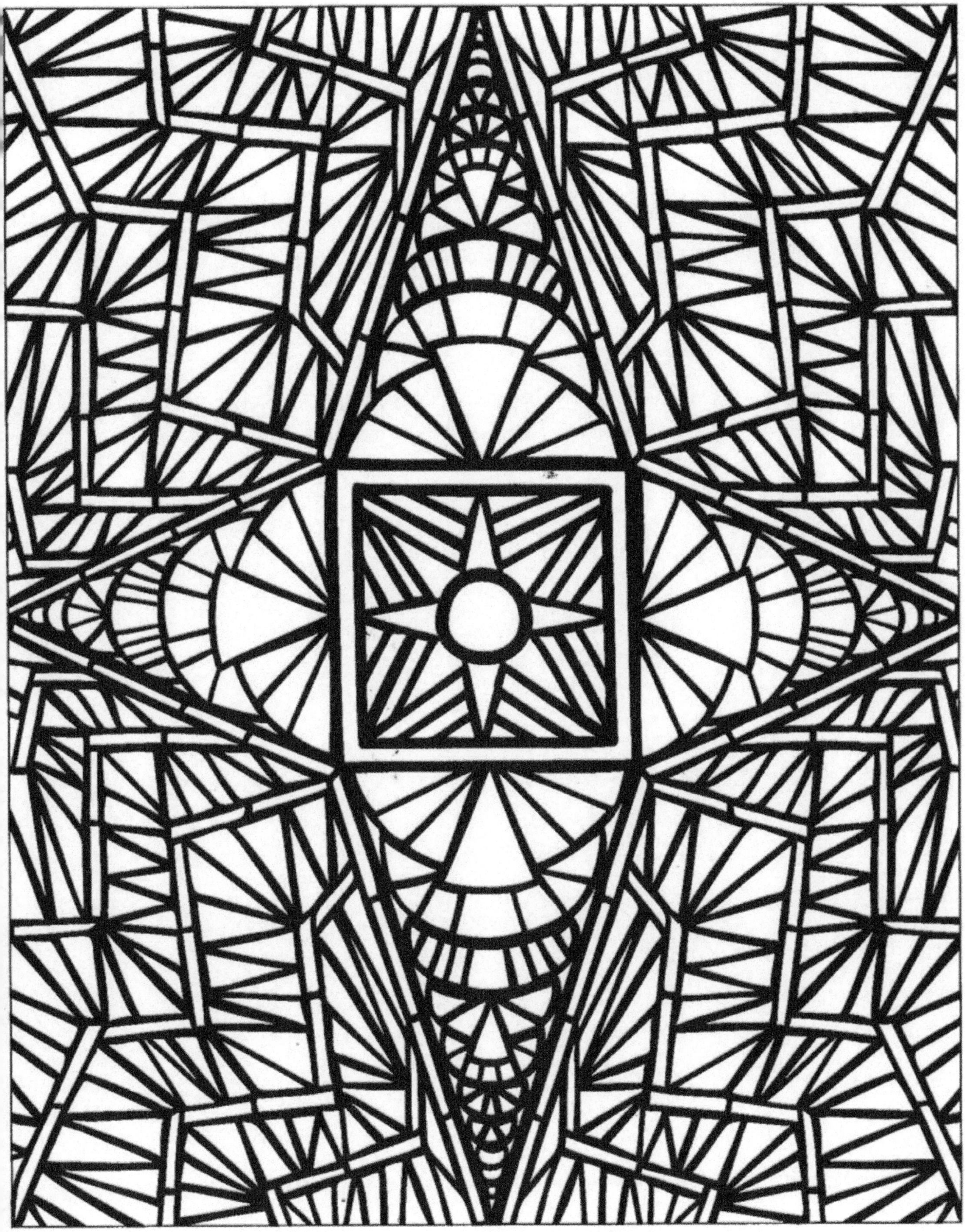

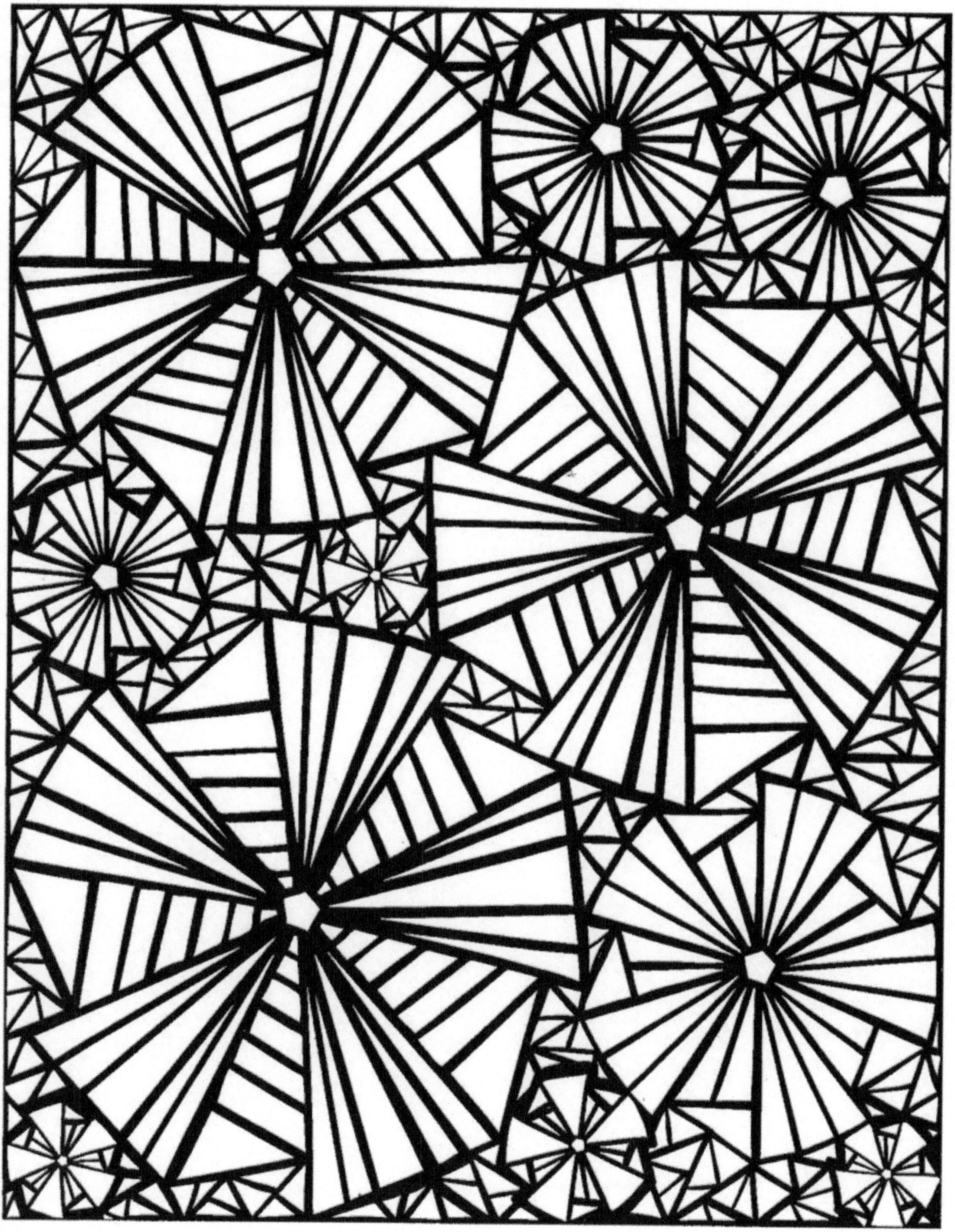

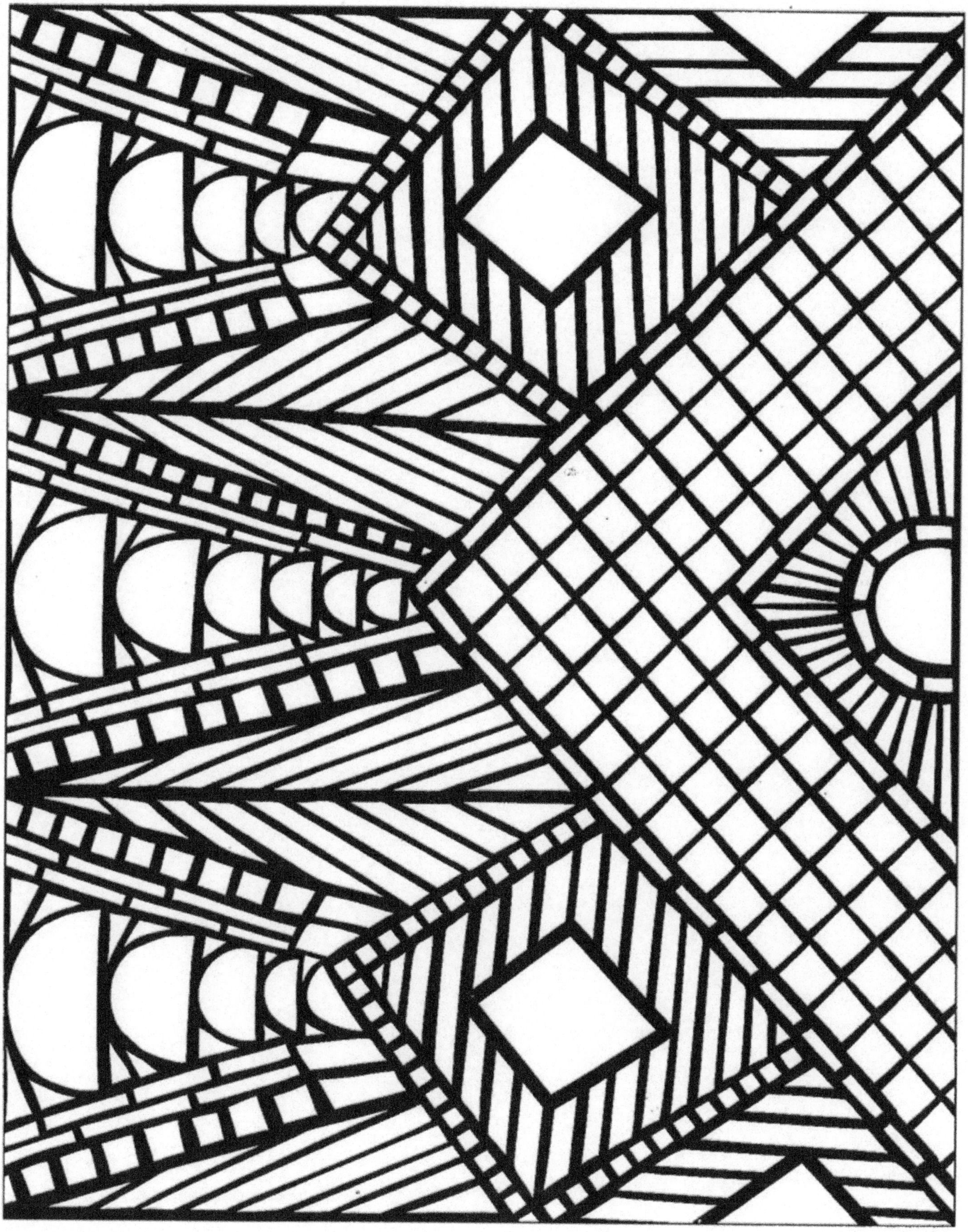

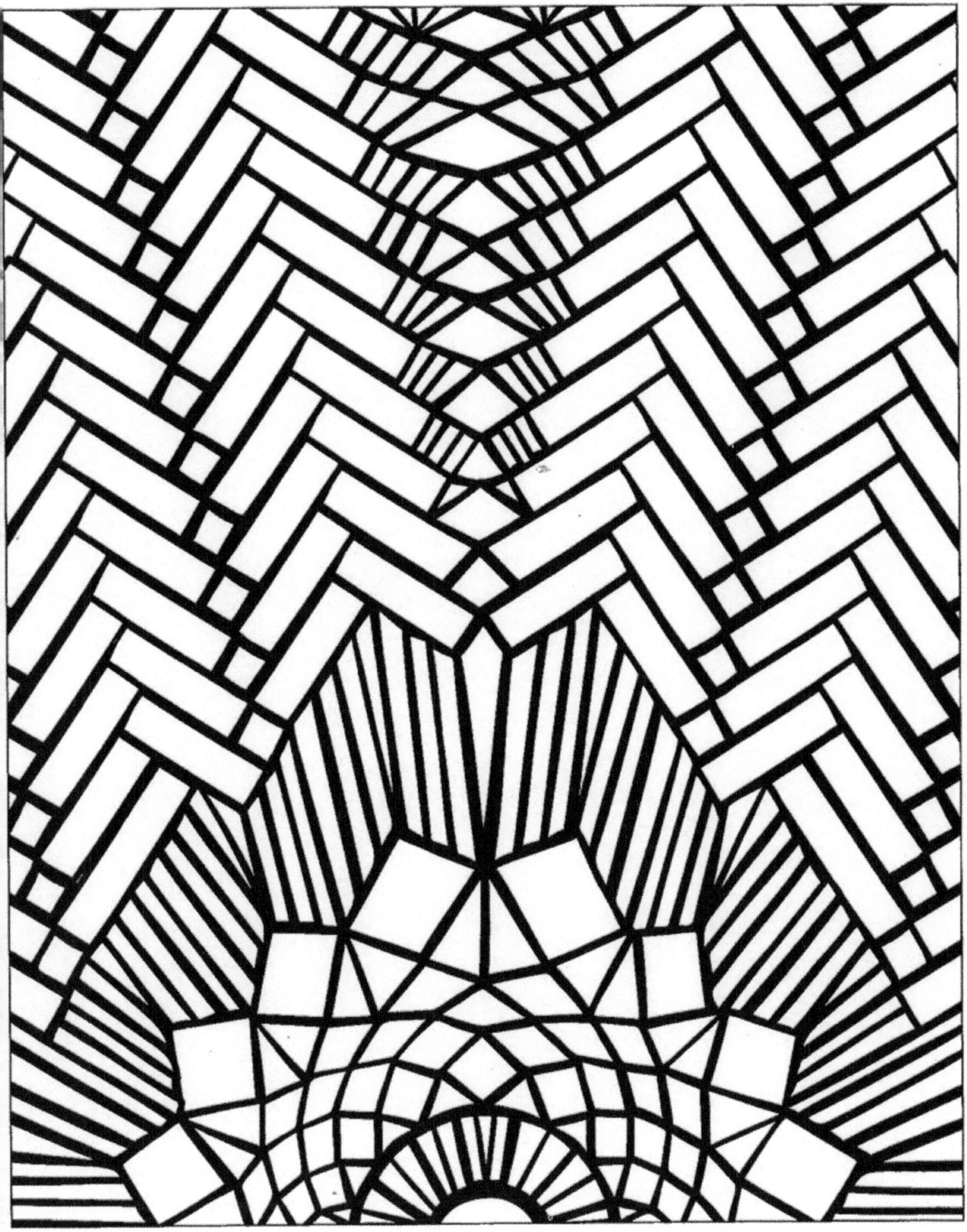

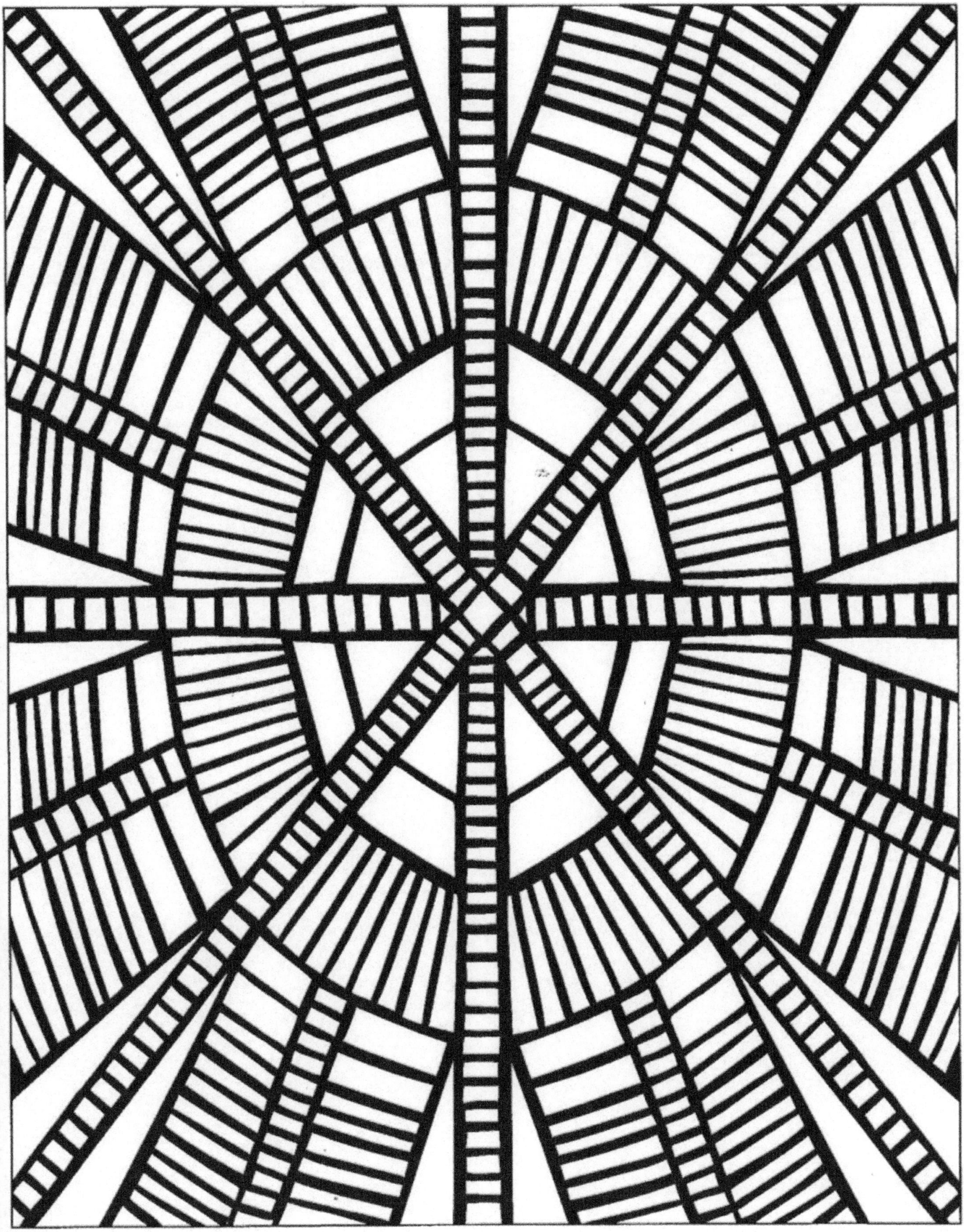

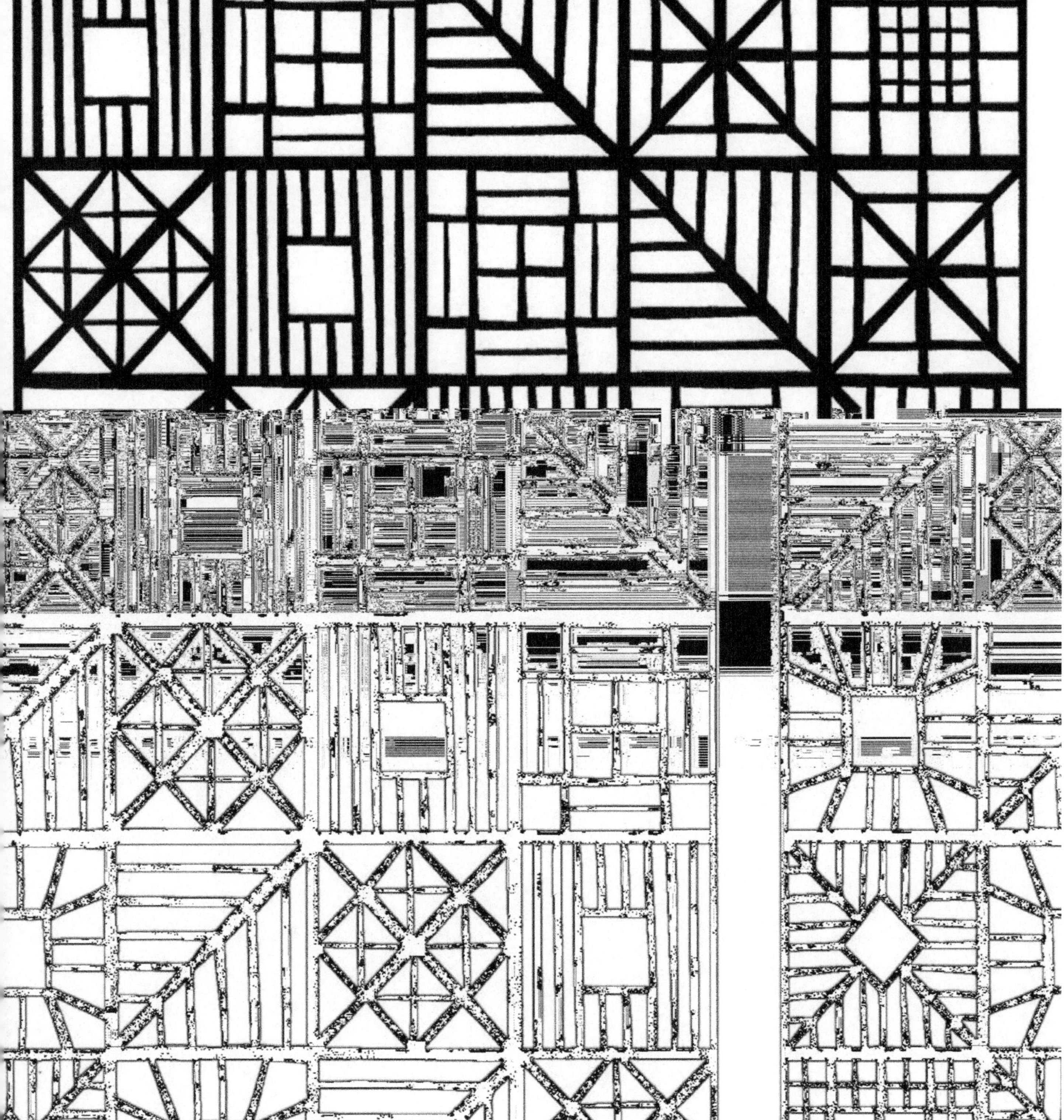

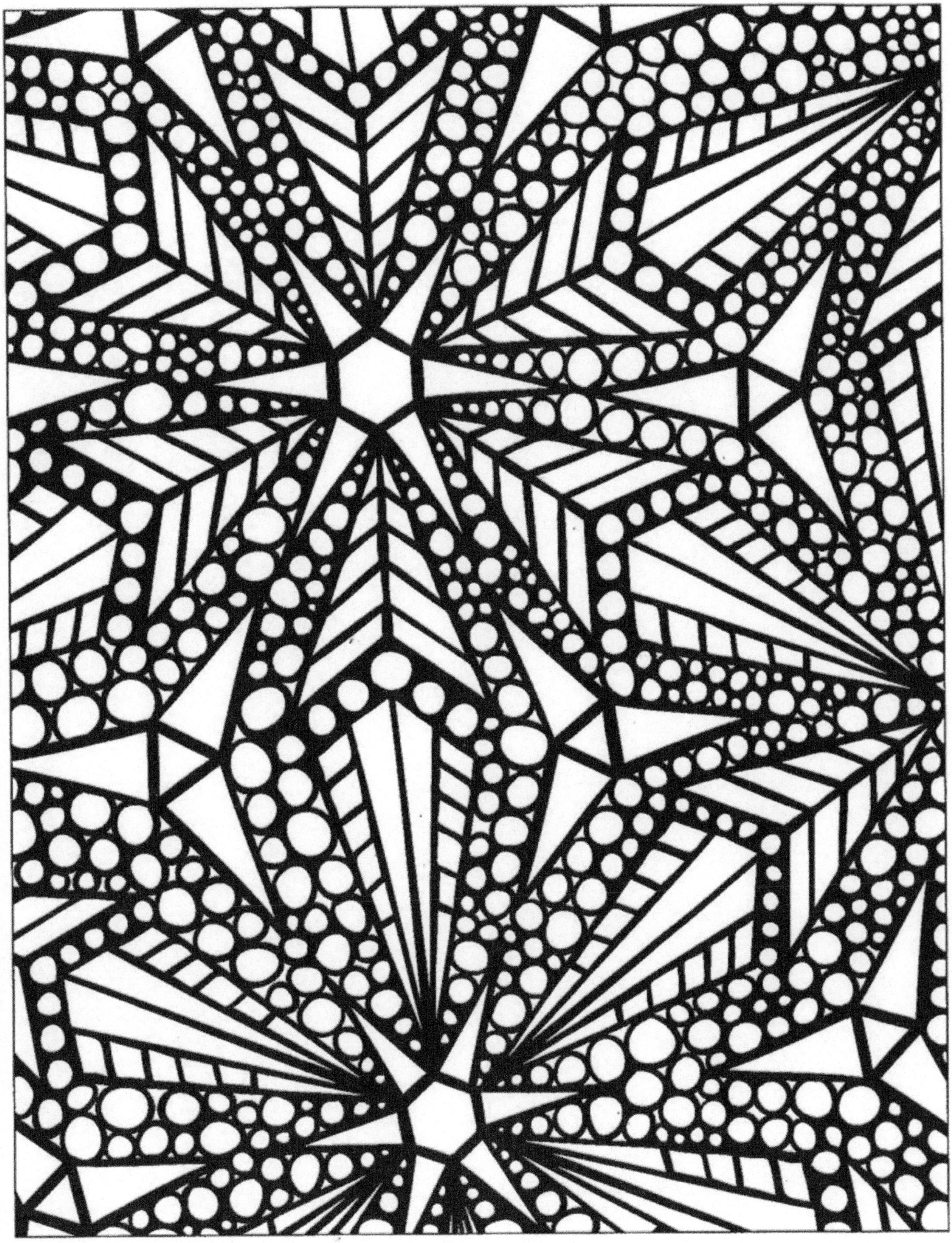

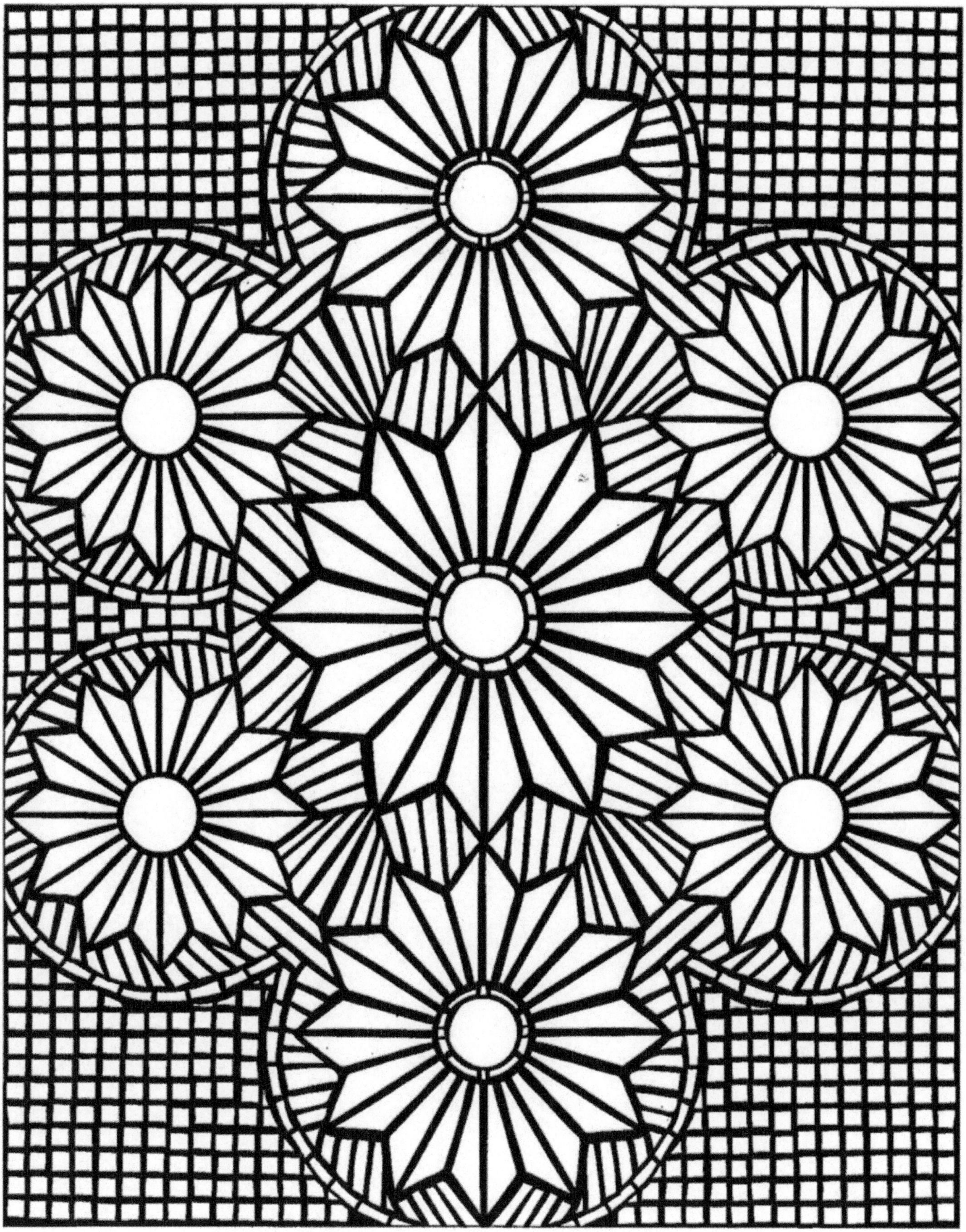

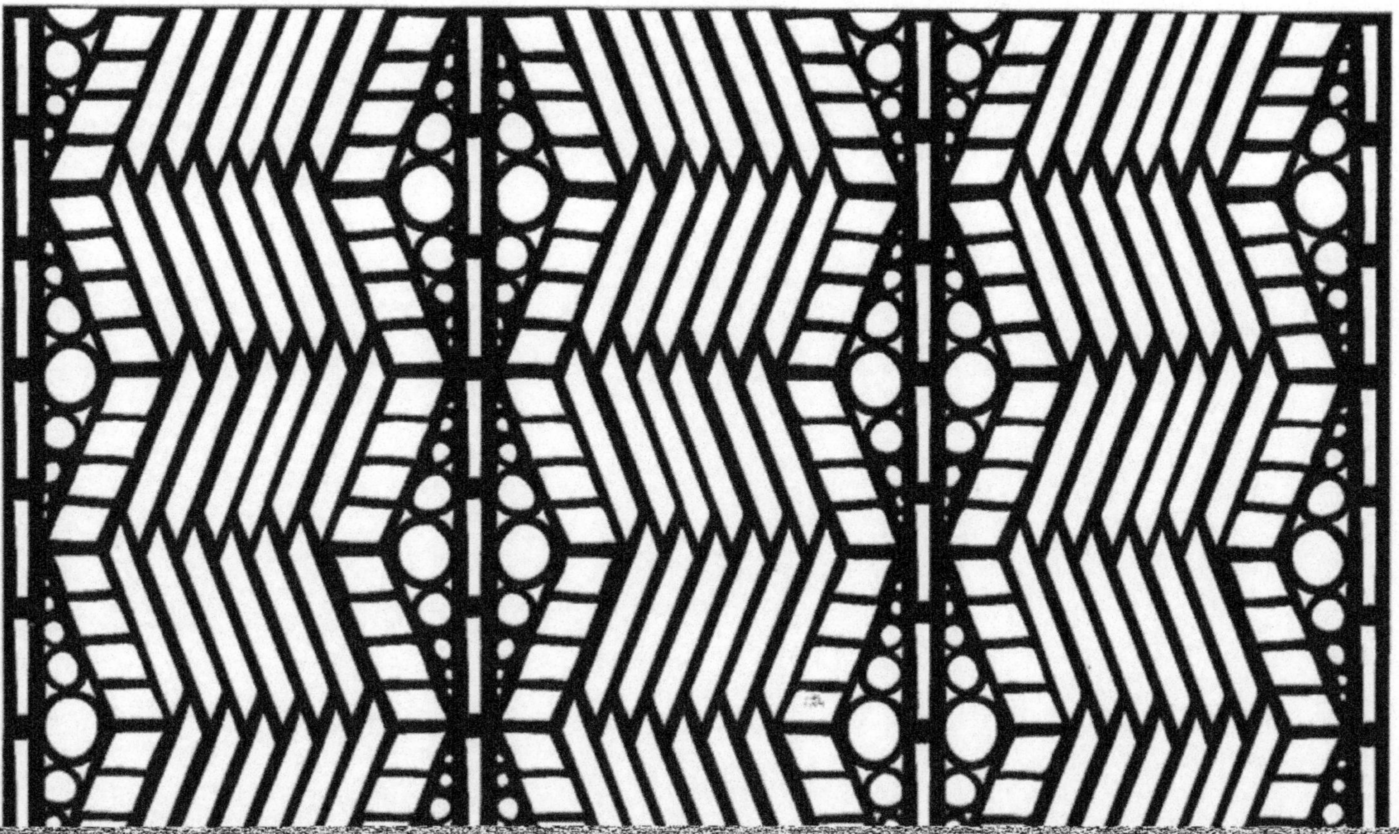

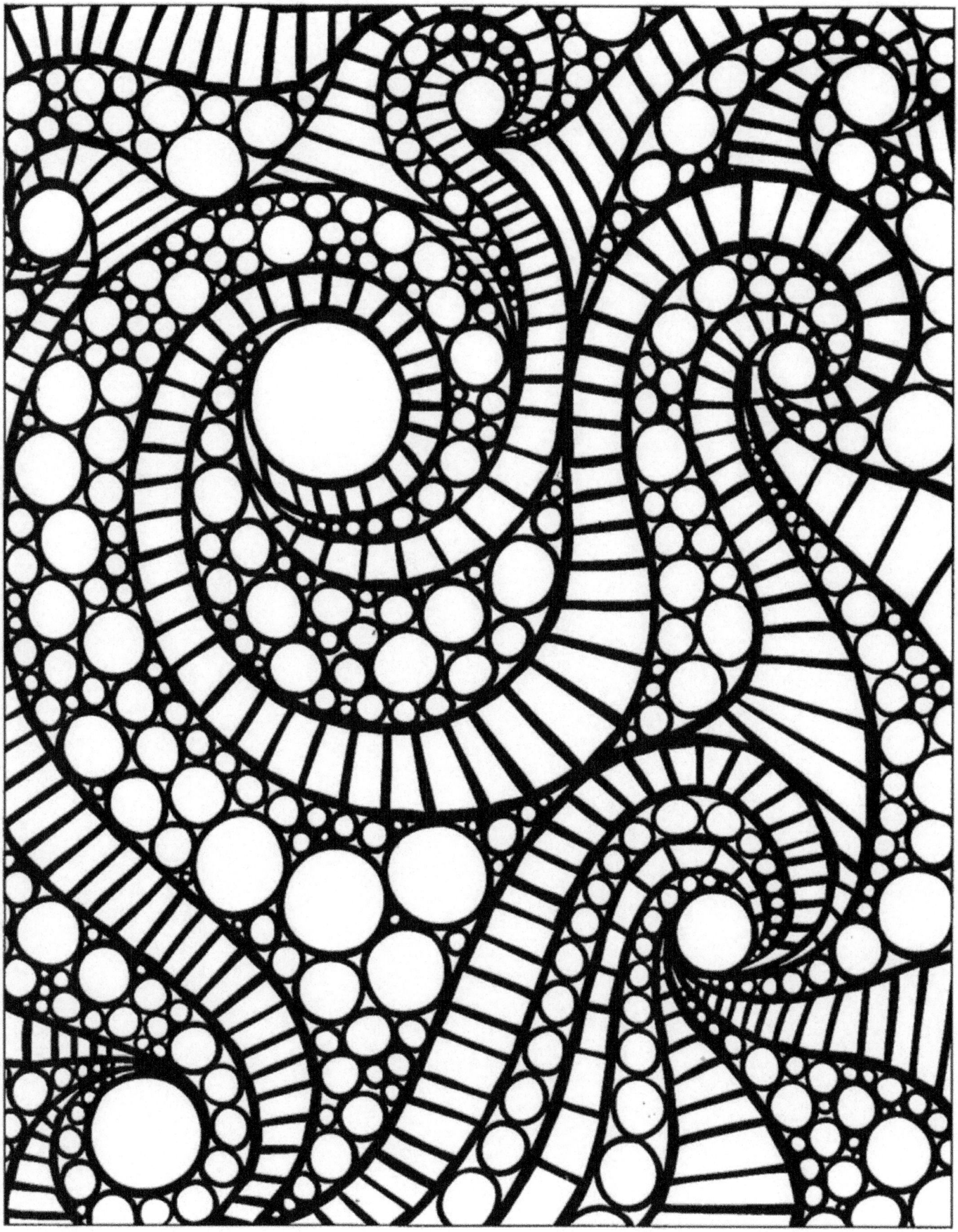

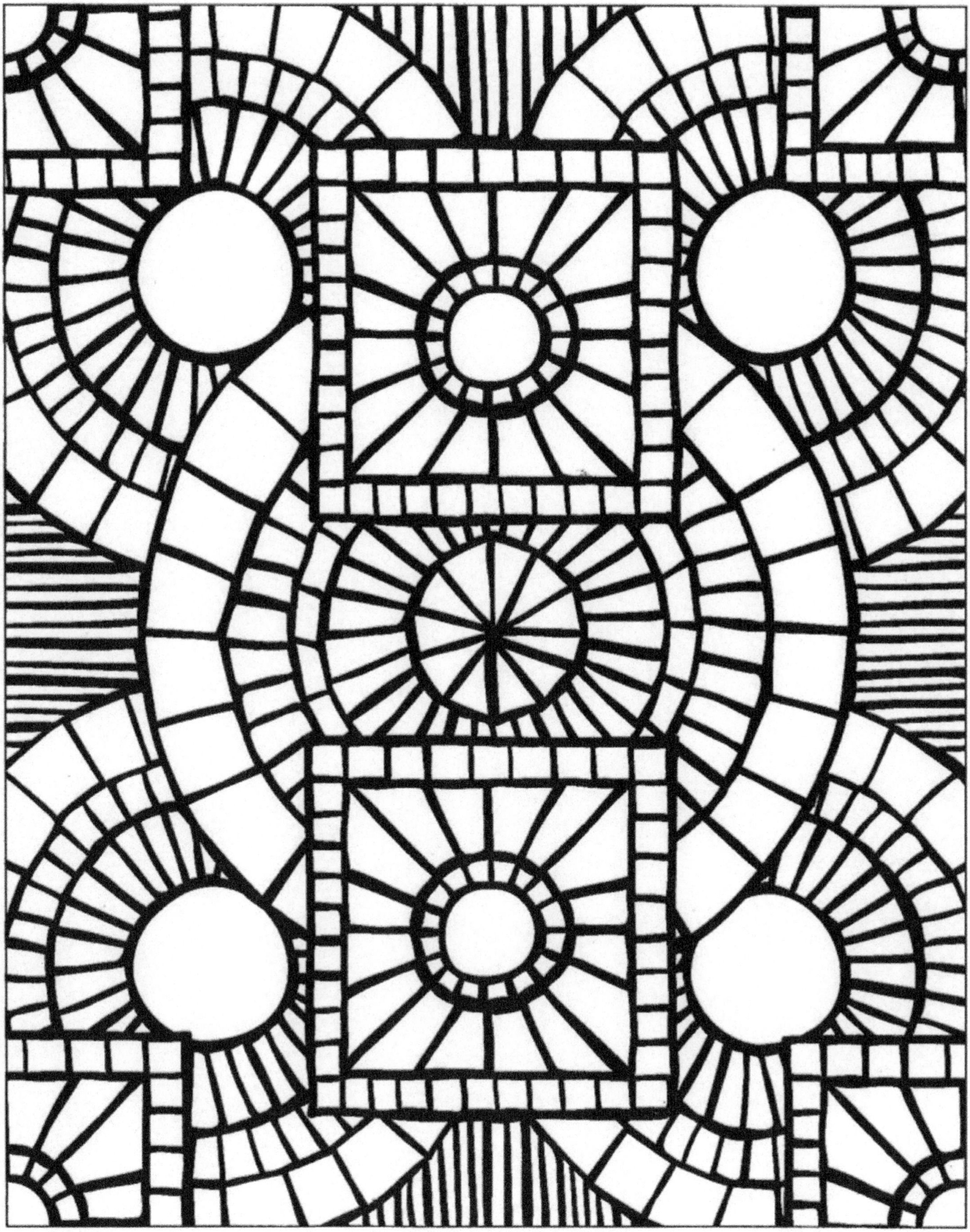

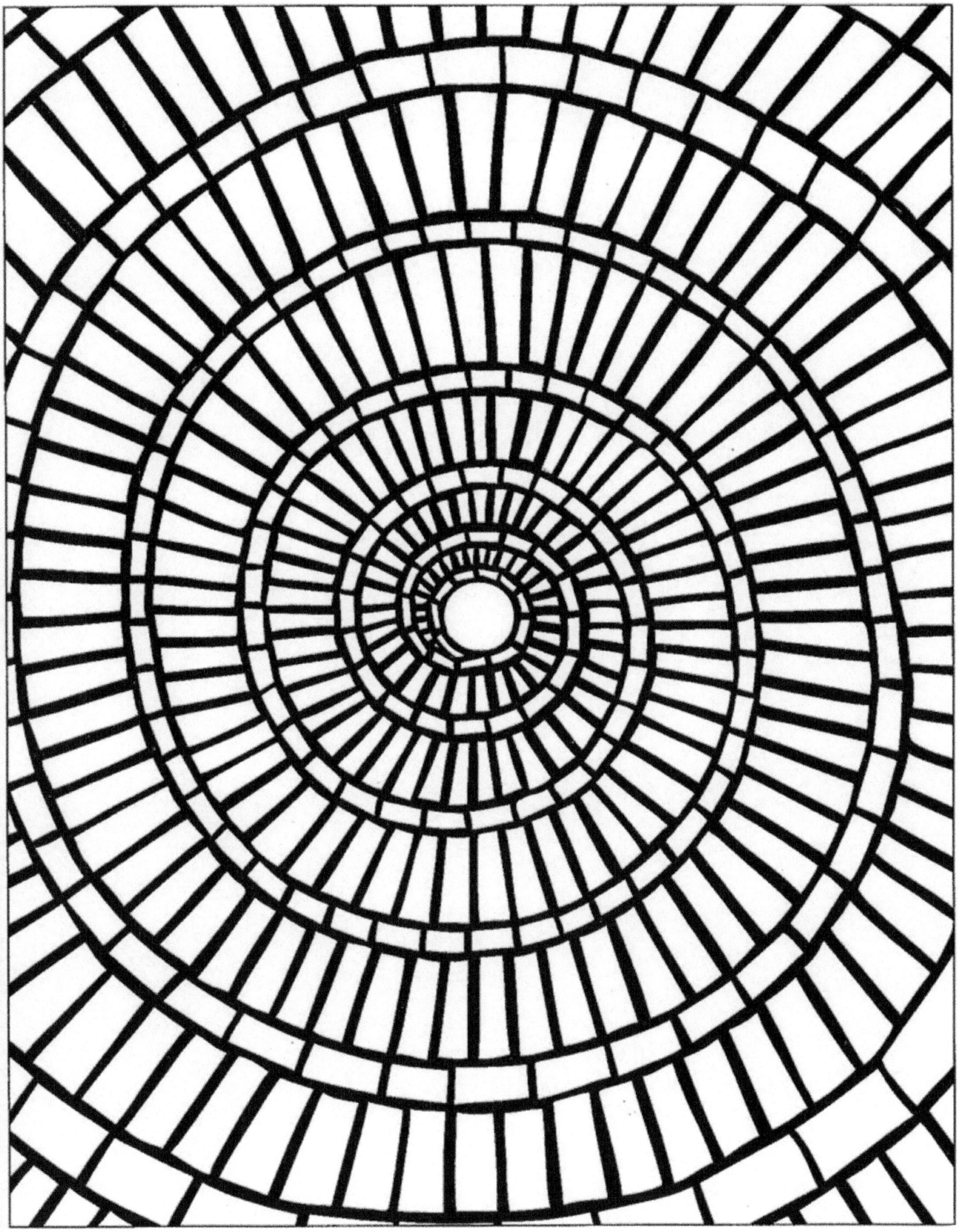

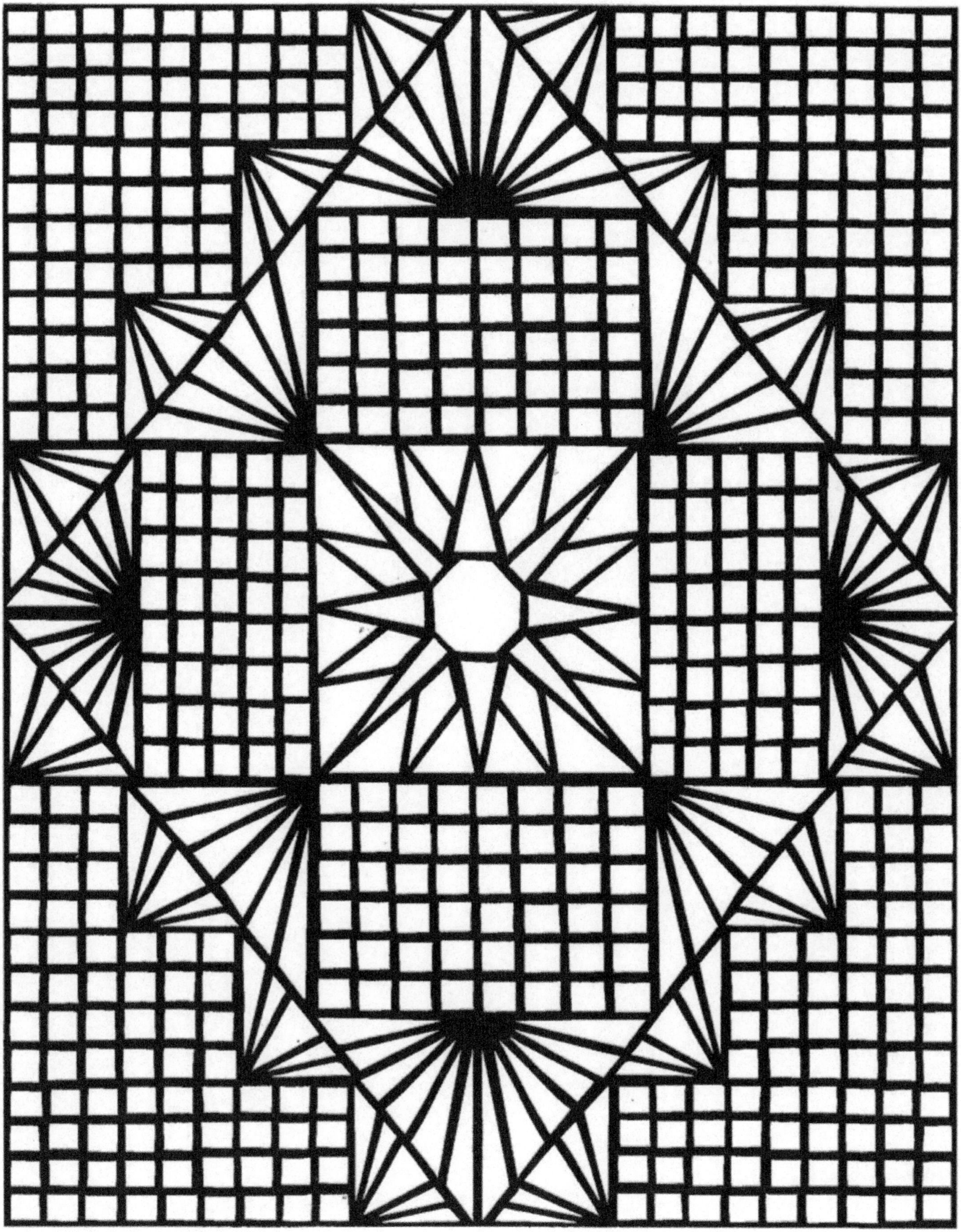

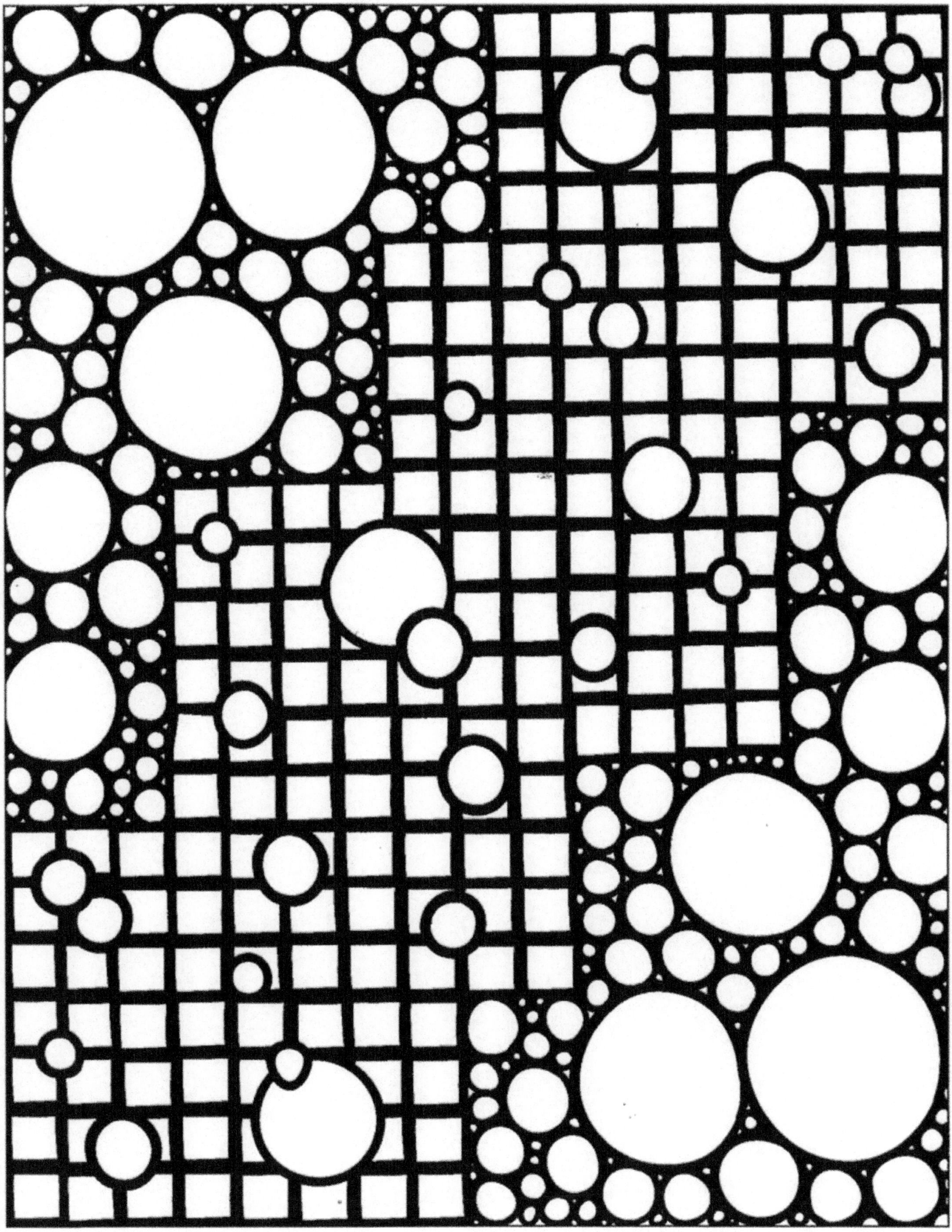

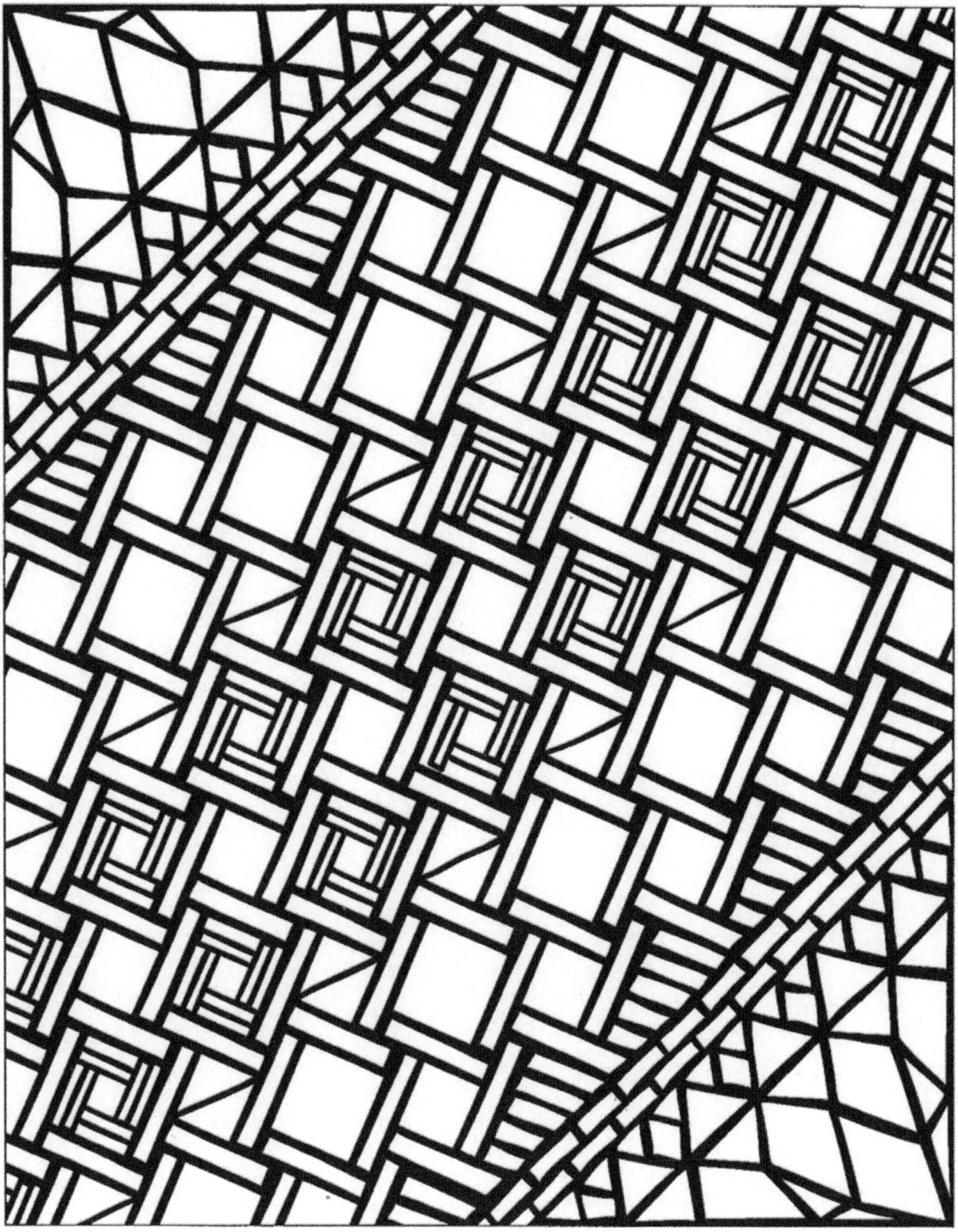

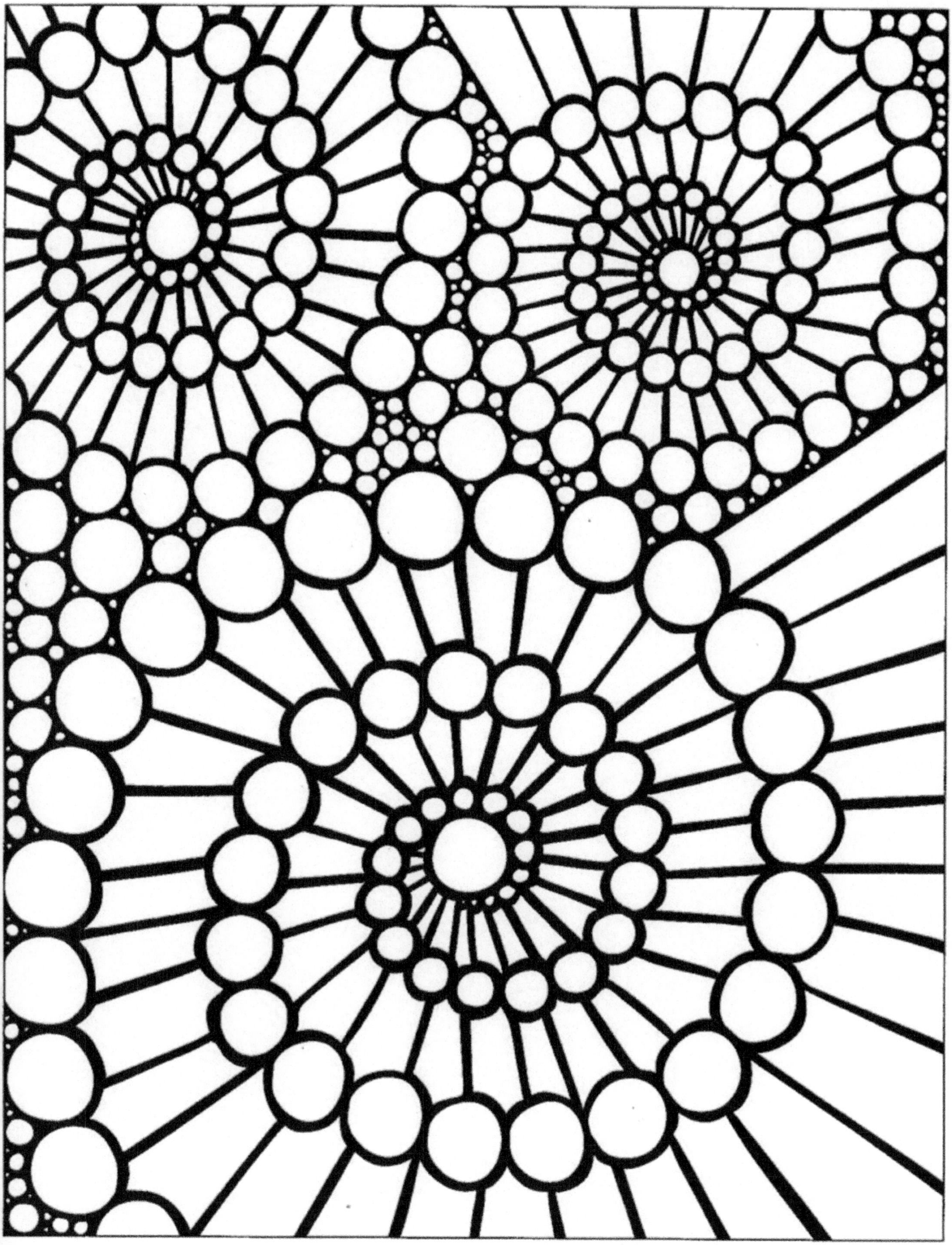

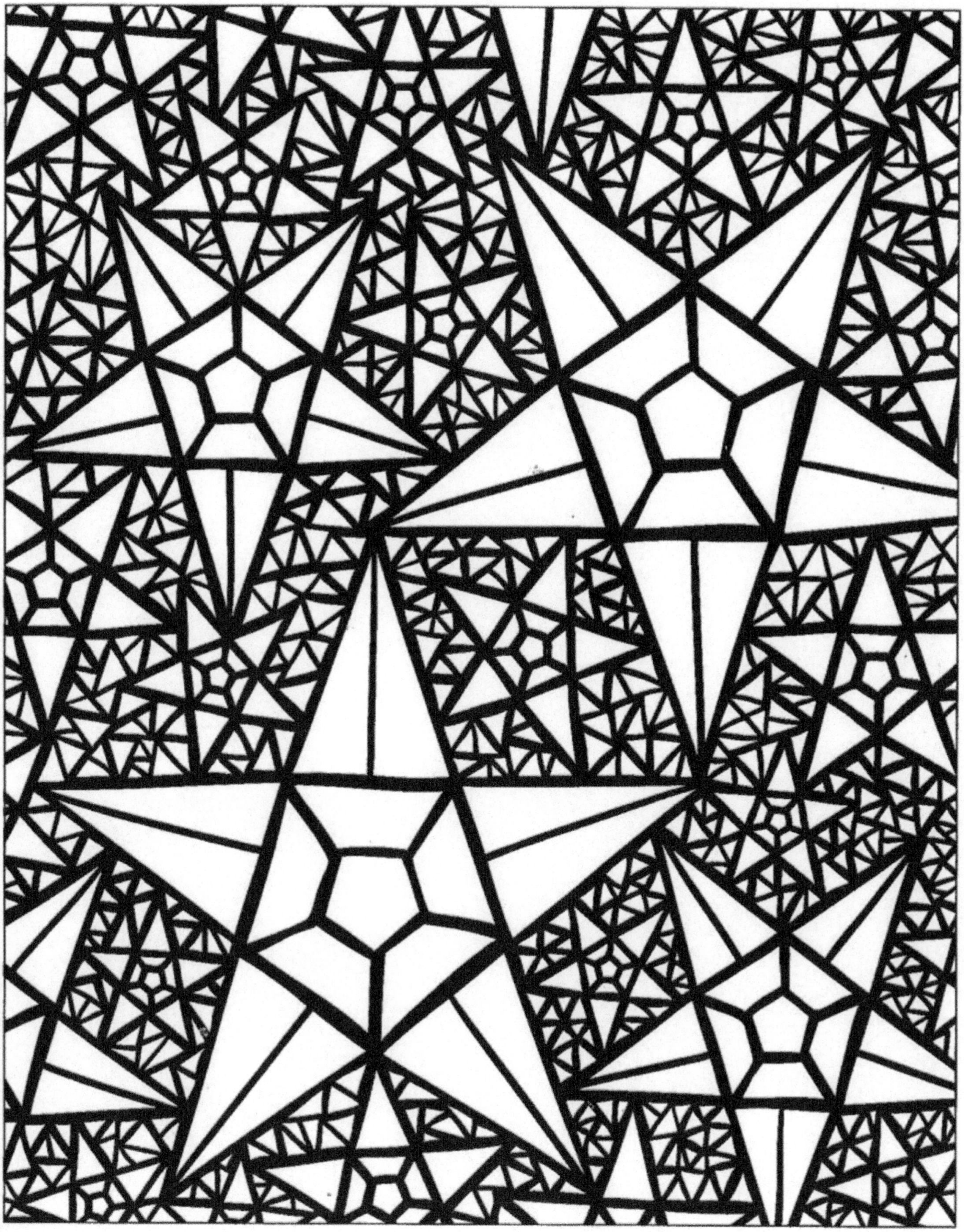

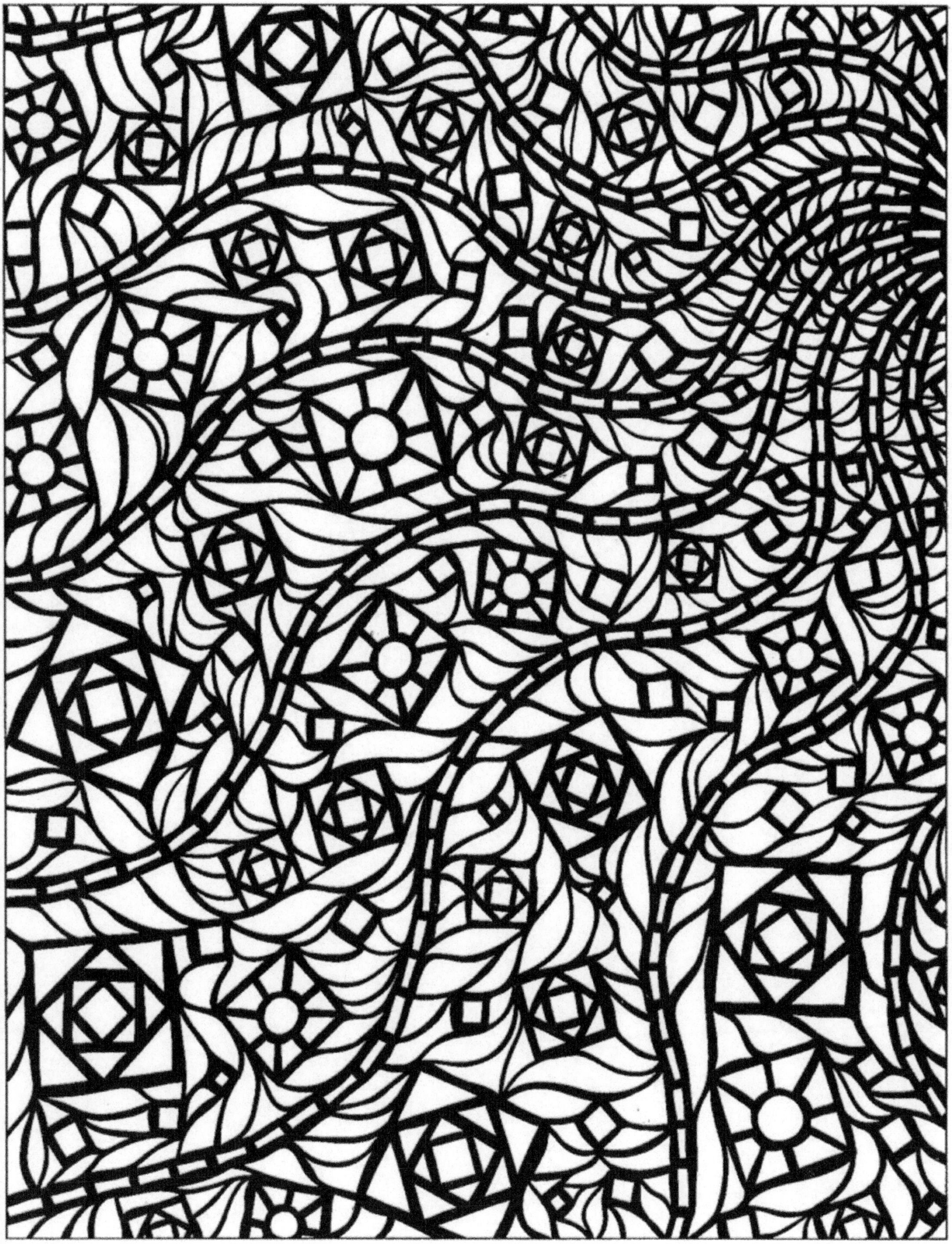

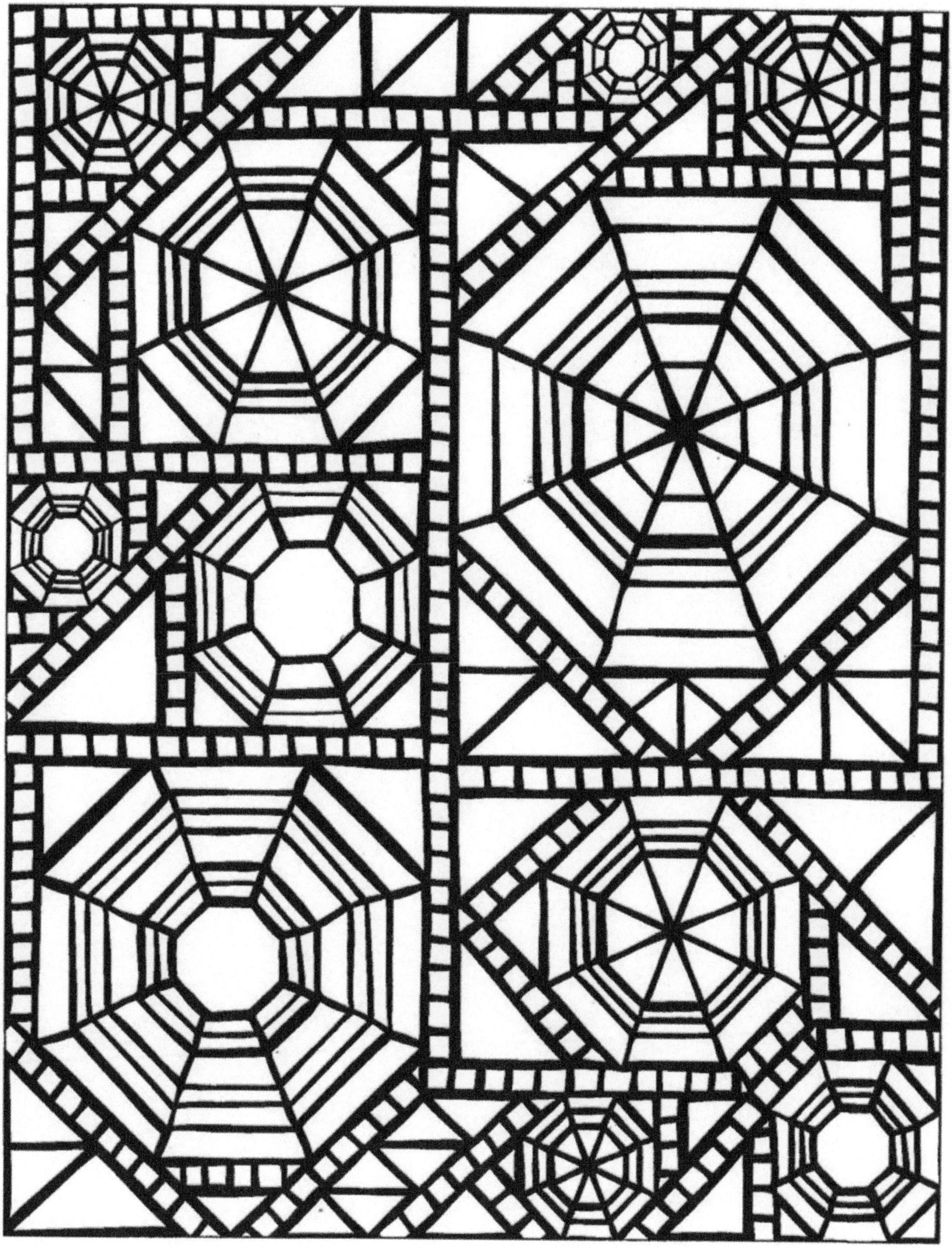

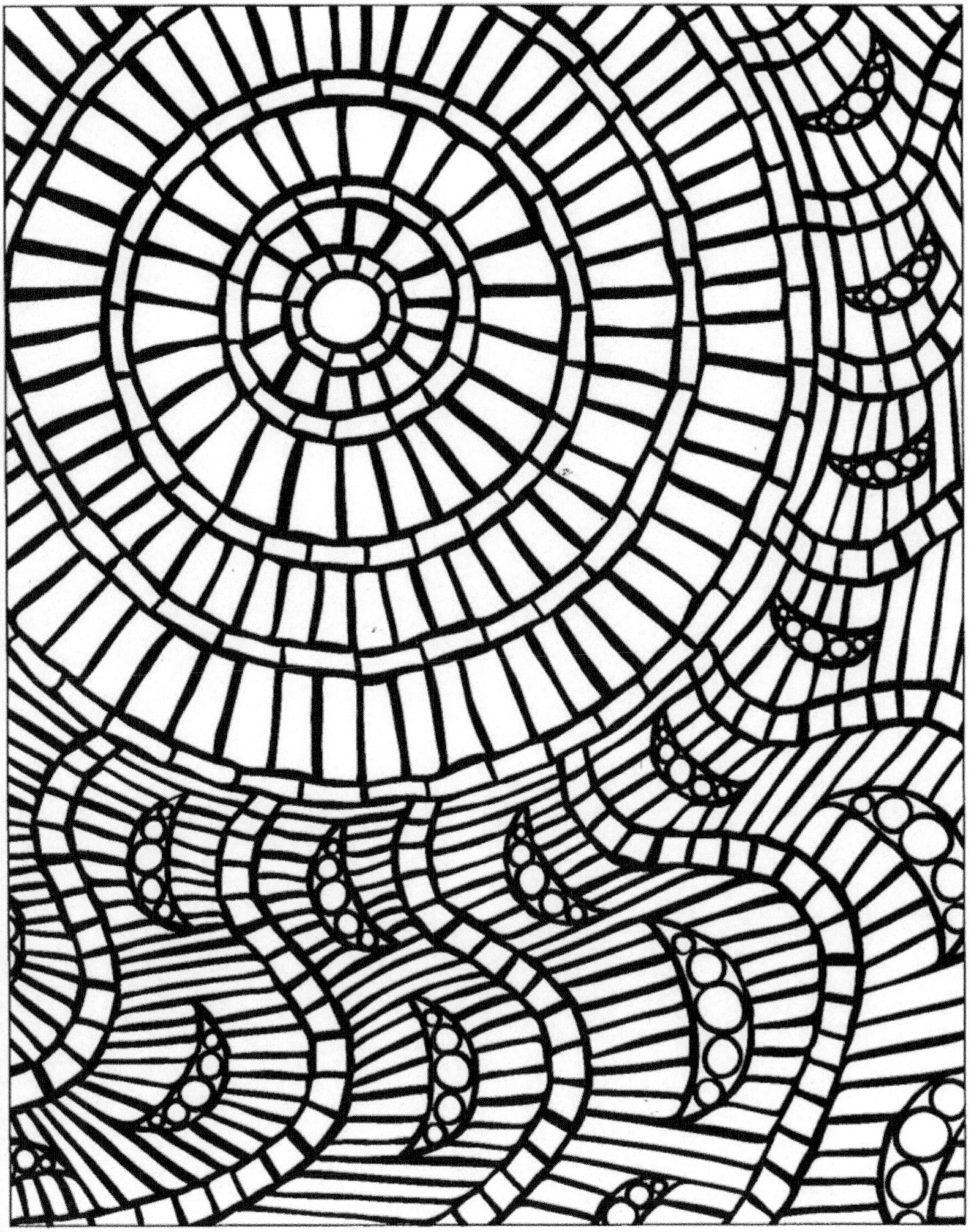

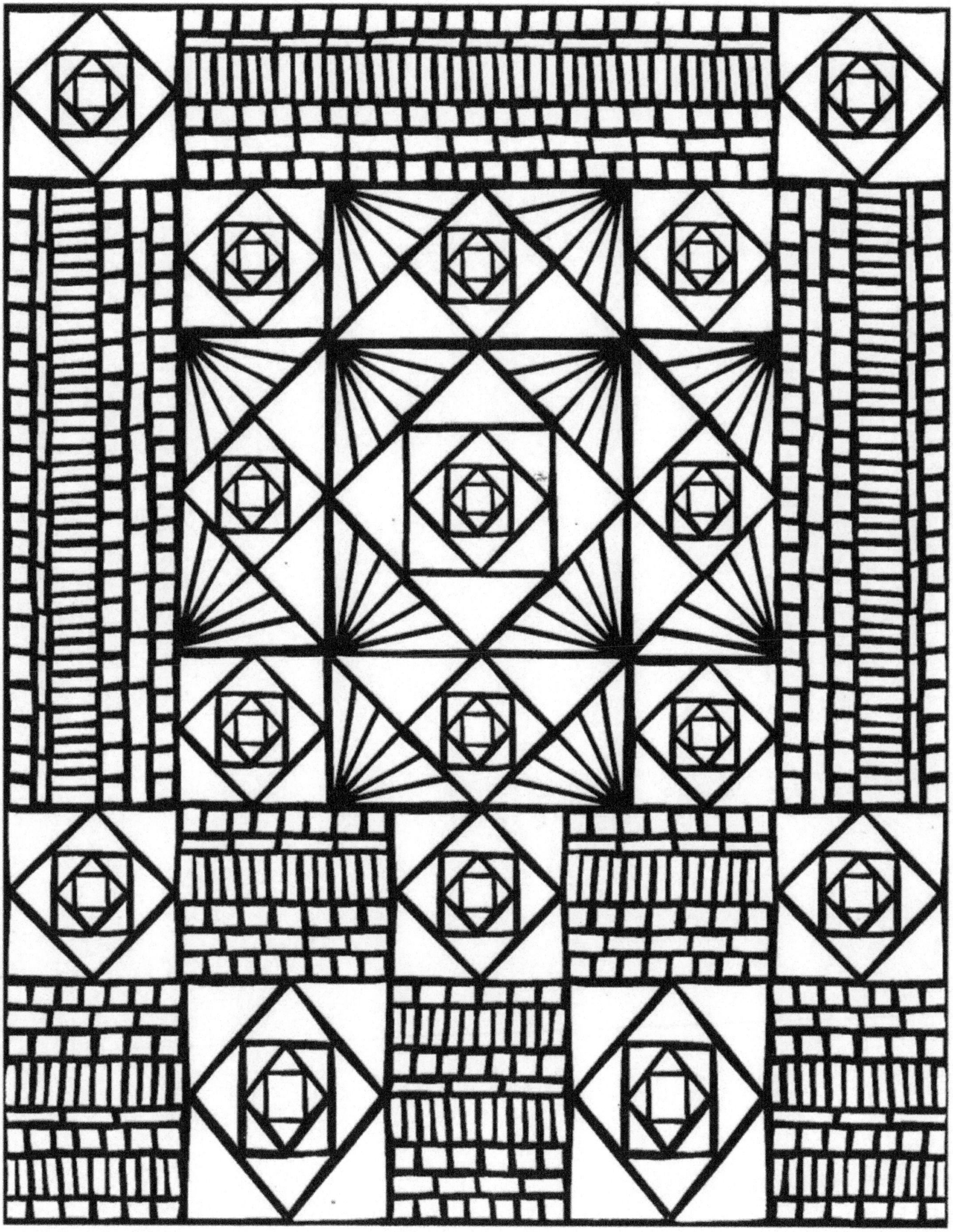

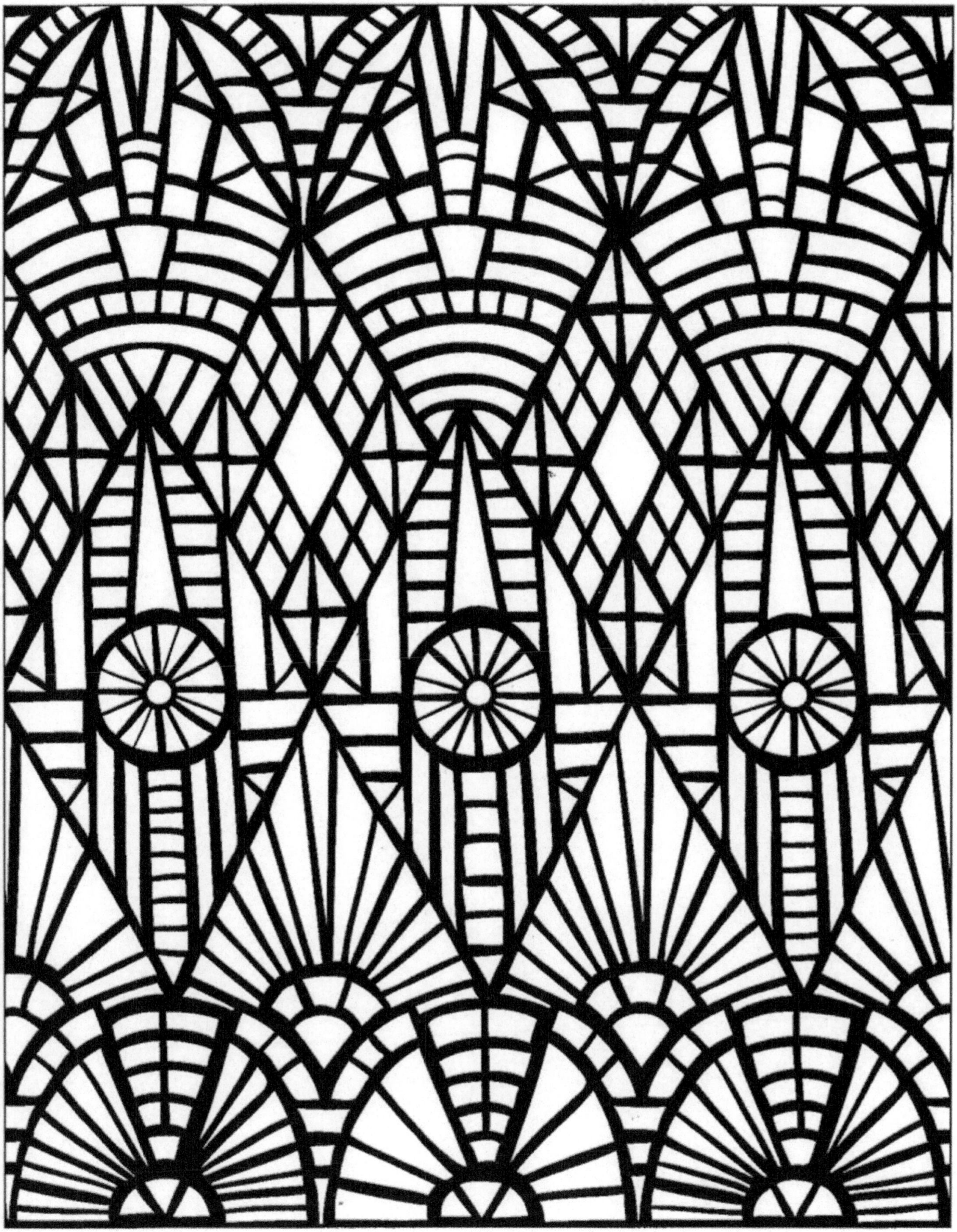

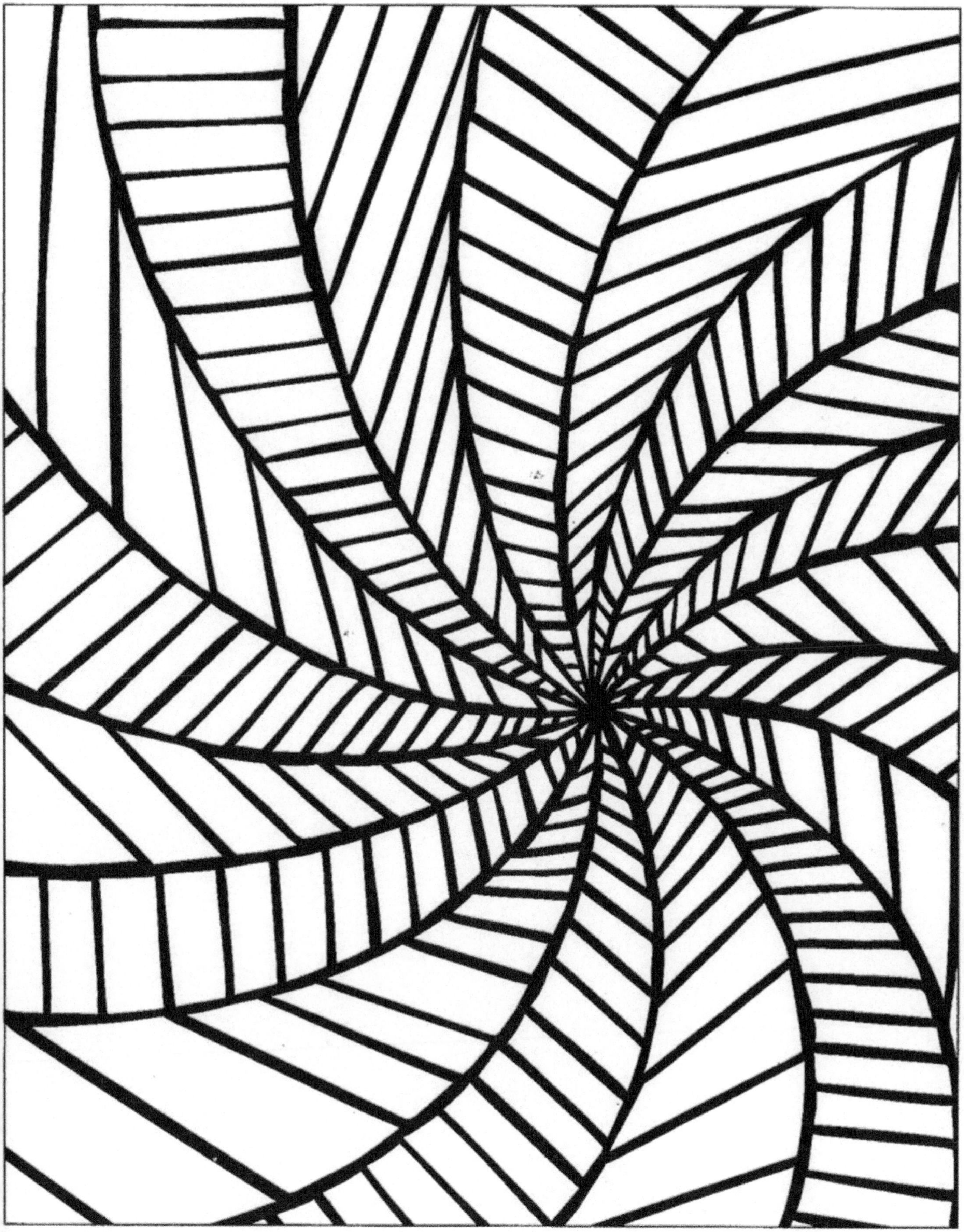

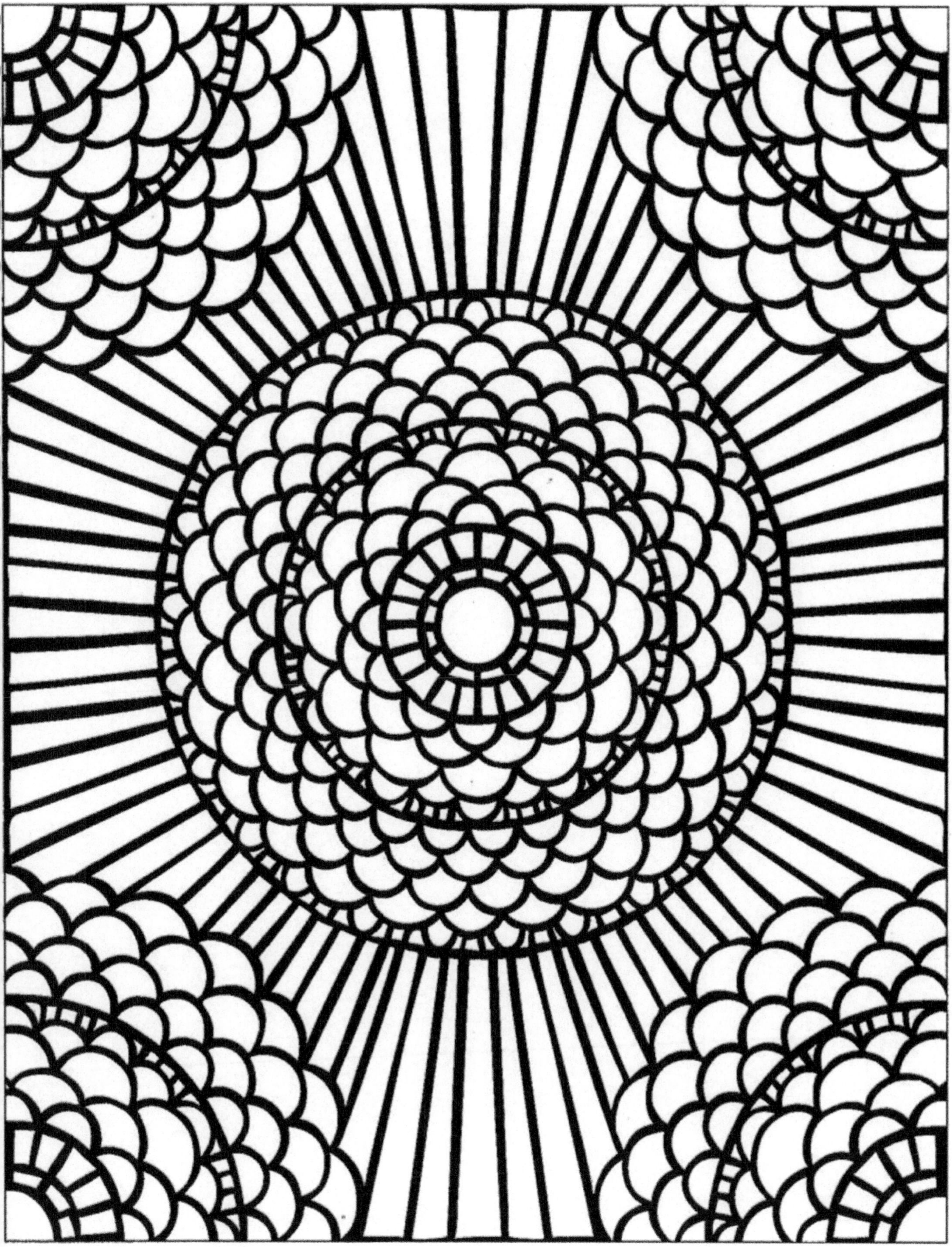

Printed in Great Britain
by Amazon

42767897R00037